WELCOME TO THE WORLD OF ANIMALS

Foxes

Diane Swanson

Gareth Stevens Publishing
A WORLD ALMANAC EDUCATION GROUP COMPANY

Please visit our web site at: www.garethstevens.com
For a free color catalog describing Gareth Stevens Publishing's list of high-quality books
and multimedia programs, call 1-800-542-2595 (USA) or 1-800-387-3178 (Canada).
Gareth Stevens Publishing's fax: (414) 332-3567.

The publishers acknowledge the support of the Canada Council for the Arts and the Cultural Services
Branch of the Government of British Columbia in making this publication possible.

The author acknowledges Matt Austin of the Ministry of Environment, Lands and Parks in British
Columbia for reviewing this manuscript.

Library of Congress Cataloging-in-Publication Data

Swanson, Diane, 1944-
   [Welcome to the world of foxes]
   Foxes / by Diane Swanson. — North American ed.
     p. cm. — (Welcome to the world of animals)
   Includes index.
   Summary: An introduction to the physical characteristics, behavior, habitat, and life cycle
of the foxes, emphasizing the development of fox pups.
   ISBN 0-8368-3562-X (lib. bdg.)
   1. Foxes—Juvenile literature. [1. Foxes.] I. Title.
QL737.C22S824   2003
599.775—dc21   2002030283

This edition first published in 2003 by
Gareth Stevens Publishing
A World Almanac Education Group Company
330 West Olive Street, Suite 100
Milwaukee, WI 53212 USA

This U.S. edition © 2003 by Gareth Stevens, Inc. Original edition © 1998 by Diane Swanson.
First published in 1998 by Whitecap Books, Vancouver. Additional end matter © 2003
by Gareth Stevens, Inc.

Series editor: Lauren Fox
Design: Katherine A. Goedheer
Cover design: Renee M. Bach

Cover photograph: Tim Christie
Photo credits: John Sylvester/First Light 4, 28; Wayne Lynch 6, 14, 26, 30; Herbert Lange/First Light 8;
Brian Milne/First Light 10; Tim Christie 12, 20, 24; Thomas Kitchin/First Light 16; Lynn M. Stone 18;
Aubrey Lang 22

Printed in the United States of America

1 2 3 4 5 6 7 8 9 07 06 05 04 03

Contents

World of Difference

Furry and bushy-tailed, foxes are handsome members of the dog family. They are cousins of the wolf and just as wild, but smaller. Five large foxes weigh less than one large wolf.

Around the world, there are about twenty kinds of foxes. In North America, there are four main kinds, each with perky ears, a pointed snout, and a long tail.

The largest and most common foxes are red foxes, which aren't always red. Some are gray-brown or silvery black, but most have black legs and white-tipped tails.

Next largest in size are gray foxes,

Taking life easy, this red fox rests its head on a bed of grass.

Muffled in fluffy fur, an Arctic fox sleeps warmly in freezing weather.

which have salt-and-pepper coats and black-tipped tails. To spot a gray fox, you might have to look up. Long claws on their back feet help them climb trees.

Smaller Arctic foxes are usually white in winter to blend with the snow, but some are ice blue. In summer, their coats turn brown to blend with the ground.

Arctic foxes have smaller ears and shorter legs than other foxes. That means less body heat escapes from these exposed body parts. Fur on the soles of their feet helps keep them warm and makes it easier to walk on slippery ice.

North America's smallest foxes are the size of large house cats, and they are mostly gray in color. They are called swift foxes because of the speed they use to chase jackrabbits, running faster than cars drive in cities. A swift fox is sometimes called a kit, desert, or prairie fox.

CATTY DOG

When does a dog look and act like a cat? When the dog is a fox! It peers at the world through bright cat eyes with narrow, upright pupils. It creeps low like a cat, placing its back feet carefully where its front feet have just been. It twitches its tail, then springs into the air and lands lightly — just like a cat. But all that's not too surprising. A fox and a cat need many of the same skills — they're both master mouse-catchers.

7

Where in the World

Foxes live almost everywhere — from seashores to forests and from deserts to frozen lands. Some make their homes in the quiet of the wilderness. Others live in the bustle of the big city.

The Arctic fox lives in the region all around the Arctic Ocean. Its thick coat keeps it warm, especially when it curls up as a furry ball. This fox usually hunts along coasts and on thick ice that covers parts of the ocean in winter. If it must, it will travel long distances for food. Some Arctic foxes have traveled more than 1,250 miles (2,000 kilometers) to new hunting grounds.

To escape enemies, a surefooted gray fox pup climbs a tree.

9

Except for thick woods and deserts, the red fox lives across Canada, the United States, Europe, Asia, Australia, New Zealand, and part of North Africa. It is so adaptable that it has even spread into the Arctic wilderness. Red foxes have also learned how to live close to people on farms and in towns.

For this red fox pup, the city is the place to live. Traffic is the greatest danger it faces.

The gray fox is adaptable, too. Because it is a climber, the gray fox prefers to make its home in the woods. There, it leaps from tree to tree and runs along thick branches. The gray fox lives in the United States, Mexico, Central America, and parts of Canada and South America.

The dry lands of the western United States are home to the swift fox. It also lives in parts of southern Canada. Like the gray and Arctic fox, the swift fox lives in fewer places now than it once did.

OUT ON THE TOWN

When red foxes come to the city, they make themselves at home on golf courses, in cemeteries, and in parks. But one fox was recently found where none had been seen before. It was running among the busy crowds and bright lights of a huge, downtown shopping center.

No one knows how the fox got there, but all the excitement must have worn it out. When it was moved to a quiet wildlife shelter, it slept for almost a week.

World Full of Food

Listening and smelling, the fox is on the hunt. It can hear the footsteps of a beetle walking in the grass. It can sniff the scent of a rabbit, hours after one has hopped by.

The fox sees well, too, but it hunts mostly at night, depending more on its ears and nose. It often hunts small animals, such as mice and insects, but it is not fussy. It eats nearly anything it finds, including eggs, nuts, and grass. When a fox finds more than it can eat, it buries some of the food for later.

In cities, the red fox adds pet food and compost to its menu. It raids garbage cans for popcorn and bits of pizza. It steals

"Got it," this red fox pup seems to say, planting its paws firmly on a pheasant.

13

Leap. Pounce. This Arctic fox is hunting a lemming it smells under the snow.

blueberries and other food from gardens. Stepping lightly across freshly watered lawns, it sniffs and listens for earthworms that have left their burrows. In one night, it might swallow 150 wriggling worms.

The swift fox hunts fast-running rabbits, but it also makes meals of tiny animals. It gobbles up masses of grasshoppers in the summer. The gray fox, however, prefers to dine heavily on summer plants.

The Arctic fox often hunts mouselike animals called lemmings. In winter, it sniffs the lemmings in their tunnels under the snow. Then the fox dives in, feet first, to catch them.

Sometimes the Arctic fox also eats leftovers from another animal's meal. It may even follow a hunting polar bear, then wait around for any scraps left behind.

To Catch a Mouse

The patter of tiny feet in the grass stops a fox in its tracks. Silent and still, it sniffs and waits to hear the patter again. Then it creeps s-l-o-w-l-y toward the sound.

As the fox gets close, the patter stops. But the fox is quick to pounce. Leaping up and forward on its strong back legs, it lands — front legs first. Pushing its paws through the grass, the fox traps the mouse, then chomps down. Dinner is served!

World of Words

Foxes growl and foxes howl. They talk like pet dogs, using many of the same sounds and actions.

Because foxes spend a lot of time alone, they often make long-distance calls to each other. One fox might scream, "Waaaah," especially at mating times, or it might cry out, "Wow, wow, wow." From far away, another fox might answer, "Wow, wow, wow."

Back and forth the foxes call as they gradually move toward one another. When they get close, their doglike calls might change to chickenlike cluckings. The

A red fox may say hello to other foxes by SCREAMING.

A snuggle is a warm greeting in any language — including Arctic fox talk.

weaker fox might welcome the other with a high whine.

Then the foxes might let their bodies do the talking. If they're happy, they show it by wagging their tails. But if one fox wants to fight, it arches its back and snarls. The other fox might respond the same way, or it might press its body to the ground. That's fox talk for, "I don't want to fight."

Like newborn dogs, newborn foxes whine for attention. The whines turn to barks as the pups grow older, and if they need help, they yelp. But when pups are contented, they make soft, trilling sounds.

A parent fox "huffs" to welcome its pups and coughs to warn them of danger. If the pups are not close by, the parent barks instead. The pups don't waste time answering. They just leap for safety.

SMELL ME A STORY

A fox talks through smells. It sprinkles urine near its den to say, "This place is mine." After it eats stored food, it sometimes sprays urine where the food had been. It is a smelly reminder that the "cupboard" is now empty.

When it waves its tail, a fox releases scent from a small tail gland. Sometimes the scent smells like violets. Scientists aren't sure exactly what the smell is saying, but foxes share it most often at mating times.

New World

Newborn foxes look nothing like their parents. They don't have pointed fox faces. Instead, their snouts are short and rounded. The color of their fur is usually quite different from the adults' fur. Red foxes may be born with woolly brown coats; gray foxes, with black ones.

The number of newborns in a fox family varies a lot, but it's usually four to six. As you might expect, the pups are very small. At birth, the largest kind of fox — the red — weighs only as much as a lemon.

A mother fox finds a safe, dry den in which to give birth to her pups. It may be a

Red fox pups emerge from a den that they may share with another fox family.

From its cozy underground burrow, a gray fox peeks out at the world.

hollow log or an empty cave. It may be a tunnel she digs herself or a burrow that was dug by some other animal. The climbing gray fox may pick a spot high in a hollow tree.

Whatever den she chooses, the mother fox usually returns to the same one each year. But before she has more pups, she may work to make her home bigger and better.

At birth, the tiny fox pups snuggle helplessly together. They can't hear, and they can't see. Their mother stays with them day and night, keeping them safe, warm, and clean. She feeds the hungry pups her rich milk. The father fox hunts for food to feed his mate, delivering it right to the den.

After a few weeks, the fox pups are able to leave the den. They spend most of their time playing, eating, and sleeping — all under the watchful eyes of their parents.

AT HOME IN THE ARCTIC

It's hard to dig a den if the ground is frozen. Arctic foxes search riverbanks and hills for sandy soil they can burrow into. But they may have to use a rock pile for a home.

Underground Arctic fox dens are usually sets of tunnels with four to twelve openings. Huge dens may have as many as one hundred openings. The dens are easy to spot because the grass above them is so healthy. All that digging by foxes helps the grass grow.

Small World

Fox pups can't spend all day just playing. They have to learn how to hunt, too. They watch their parents closely and try hard to imitate them.

A hunting lesson might begin with a parent bringing home a dead bird. The pup sniffs the bird and rolls it across the ground. It sneaks up and pounces on the bird, then tosses it about. Finally, the pup might fight with another pup for the bird. In later lessons, the parents might bring home a bird that is still alive.

The pup is soon ready to follow its parents on hunting trips. It must learn what

When they're away from the den, red fox pups stay where it's safe — close to a parent.

A swift fox checks out its pups. Big ears and a black-tipped tail are common among these foxes.

to eat and how to catch it. The pup usually starts to hunt by grabbing easy prey, such as slow-moving insects.

The fox pup also learns to sniff out food that its parents have stored. Just for practice, it digs up the food, then buries it again, patting the dirt back with its nose.

While the pup is busy learning, the parents are busy guarding. Foxes not only watch for enemies on the ground; they keep an eye on the sky as well. A hungry hawk might swoop down and snatch a pup. At the slightest signal from its parents, the pup shoots to safety. For a gray fox, that usually means heading up the nearest tree.

A fox is often less than a year old when it starts out on its own. If it has learned its lessons well, it may live to be ten years old.

ON THE LOOKOUT

One day, a swift fox spotted a coyote lurking near its den. The fox knew that its family was in danger. It waited until the coyote had passed, then moved its pups to a new home — an empty badger burrow. The fox dug the burrow deeper, then added more escape holes. The family was safe — for now.

Foxes of every kind are always on the lookout for enemies. Besides coyotes, they fear wolves, eagles, hawks, and people.

Fun World

Wrestling, romping, even somersaulting. Young foxes are peppy, playful pups.

One might creep through tall grass, then pounce on some make-believe prey. Or the pup might shadow a beetle or jump on a bone. It might toss a twig into the air, then spring up to catch it.

When the mother fox is resting, her pups might sneak up on her, as if they were stalking a mouse. Or they might hurl themselves across her back or scramble all over her. When she has had enough of her pups' play, she just moves a short distance away.

Sunshine and play make a fun day for these red fox pups.

29

Fox pups mostly play with other fox pups. Together, they bark and yip. They nibble each other's ears and tails. And they jump, roll, and wrestle where it is safe — close to the entrance of their den.

Before they eat, the pups often play tug-of-war, grabbing the same piece of food and p-u-l-l-ing. The winner eats the

A swift fox licks its lips and nose after downing food it grabbed in play.

prize. They play a similar game when one of them has a toy, such as an old bone or a pinecone. The other pups try to yank it away.

Races and chases are also good fox fun. If the pups try to stop fast, they may flip a few somersaults. But all that play is great exercise. It helps the pups grow strong and trains them to be hunters that are quick on their feet. The play tires them out, making them ready for sleep. Collapsing in one big pile, fox pups nestle down for a nap.

FASCINATING FOXES

Foxes have always fascinated people. Here are some reasons why:

- **Red foxes learn to cross busy city streets when the traffic is lightest.**

- **Arctic foxes live through freezing temperatures as low as -76° Fahrenheit (-60° Celsius).**

- **Swift foxes survive hot desert days in dens 3 feet (1 meter) underground.**

- **Gray foxes grip floating logs firmly enough to "sail" to nearby islands.**

Glossary

adaptable — changing easily to fit different conditions.

burrow — (n) a hole in the ground or snow, made by an animal for a home or shelter.

den — a home or shelter

emerge — to come out into view.

glands — parts of the body that produce fluid from materials in the bloodstream.

lurking — waiting out of sight or moving in a way not to be seen.

pounce — to swoop down at something and grab it.

prey — animals that are hunted by other animals for food.

pupils — the dark centers of the eyes that let light in.

scent — an odor made by an animal or plant.

signal — (n) a warning act or sound.

stalking — following very quietly.

trilling — rapid sound vibrations.

Index